Coming to Life

Coming to Life

Joy Ladin

The Sheep Meadow Press
Riverdale-on-Hudson, New York

Copyright © 2010 by Joy Ladin

Designed and typeset by The Sheep Meadow Press
Distributed by The University Press of New England

All inquiries and permission requests should be addressed to the publisher:

The Sheep Meadow Press
PO Box 1345
Riverdale, NY

Library of Congress Cataloging-in-Publication Data

Ladin, Joy, 1961–
  Coming to life / Joy Ladin.
      p. cm.
  Poems.
  ISBN 978-1-931357-83-8 (alk. paper)
  I. Title.
  PS3612.A36C66 2010
  811>.6--dc22
                                              2010030847

*For Liz, who makes life
worth coming to*

Acknowledgments

The following poems have appeared, sometimes in somewhat different forms, in the following publications:

Specs: "Coming to Life"

ANTIthesis: "The Leopard"

The Gay and Lesbian Review: "Something Else You Will Never Know About Me," "Loving Him"

LanguageAndCulture.net: "Hurting"

At-Large: "In the Water," "Survival Guide," and "Mind"

LambdaLiterary.org: "Girl in a Bottle" and "There"

Contents

I.

Growing Pain

Conclusion to a Ritual Marking the Passage
from Male to Female

All text taken from Torah verses that contain the word "joy"

Are you the city that was called the perfection of joy?
No one treads you with joy.
Although you shout, they are not shouts of joy.
Your heart knows its bitterness, and no one shares its joy.

Do not grieve for joy.
Many weep when they see this temple, while many others
        shout for joy.
No one can distinguish weeping from joy
When God has filled you with joy.

Days fly away without a glimpse of joy.
You remember how you used to go, leading the procession with
        shouts of joy.
Though you've seen deceit in the heart of joy,
You still have this consolation—in unrelenting pain, your joy.

Do not grieve for joy.
All these things you have sacrificed for joy.
The trees of the forest weep with joy,
Anointing God with the oil of joy.

God will fill your mouth with laughter and your lips with joy,
Turning and returning you to joy.
God will be your joy
When you have no glimpse of joy.

Do not grieve for joy.
The morning stars, that sing for joy,
Will remove your sackcloth and clothe you with joy.
The ache will perish in joy.

Announce this with shouts of joy:
There is joy even where there is no joy.
Swollen, throbbing with joy,
Ruins burst into songs of joy.

Do not grieve for joy.
Even sorrow shouts for joy.
When morning dawns, when evening fades, you shall have
        nothing but joy.
Those who go out weeping seed

Return with sheaves of joy.

Growing Pain

1. *Future to Past*

You
are what makes me a creature
of frustration and nightmare,
like a glass of milk
covered in hair.
Wherever you are I cease to be.
Wherever a trace of you peeps through
the prostheses of flesh and fabric
that enable me to speak
in my uniquely subjunctive mode,
in which "I" refers
to a speaker who has never existed—
first-person presumptive? projective? delusional?—
the lie of me collapses. The creature beneath—
is it me? Is it you?—
skitters into shadows lit
by the flash of corrective razors. Every day
I scrape away layers of you,
but no matter what I do, you are there
like a caul
dragging me back toward the womb
where you can unmake me, once and for all.
It's true—I'm a birth defect,
a perforation in your heart, a cleft in your palate,
a second head that never quite grew,
a wild animal clawing through
the battered, hairy skin of you
toward the life she never knew:
the freedom-salt of blood, the lope
toward rising moon.

2. *Past to Future*

I know you're done with me,
but I'm not done with you.

For years I held you while you grew.
For years you grew while I—

what happened to me? What happens
to the eggshell

when life breaks through
is happening to me

as you emerge, wondering
not at all

about the life
or am I death

that sheltered you.

What It's Like

Here is the self here are the houses
Here are the trees surrounding the houses
Here are their leaves they've begun to turn colors
Here is the lawn the driveway borders
Here is the self here are the houses

Here are the lives lived in the houses
Here is the lawn no one has raked it
Here is the frost that spiders the windows
Here is the head half-hidden by curtains
Here are the lives lived in the houses

Here is despair it spills from the houses
Surrounded by trees the color of illness
Here is the lawn you are too tired to rake it
Here is the driveway whose curve makes you nauseous
Here is despair it spills from the houses

Here is the nausea half-hidden by houses
Here is the tree spidered with illness
Here is the lawn it's begun to turn colors
Here is the driveway it billows like curtains
Here is the nausea half-hidden by houses

You are despair you spill from the houses
You are the tree whose leaves are an illness
You are the lawn you billow like curtains
You are the driveway whose curve makes you nauseous
You are despair you spill from the houses

Affair

The stranger you have become
        Is having an affair,
Torrid but loveless,

With the man
        I never was.
Now he's deep inside you,

A fertilized egg
        Clinging to the uterus
Of your dreams. The child I wouldn't,

Then couldn't,
        Begins to form. Like the rest
Of our lives together,

He will never be born.

The Future is Trying to Tell Us Something

For Nasia, age 3

The future is trying
to tell us something
we are trying

not to hear. It refuses
to play quietly by itself, demands we drop
everything to pick it up, stop

to brush its wisps of hair,
teach it to read
the looks of despair

we tell ourselves don't show, answer
when it tries to tell us
it doesn't know how to grow.

Something Else You Will Never Know About Me

This morning we were still in love,
rolling on a bed
that widened as we kissed.

You were twenty-five again.
I was still a man. Lit
by a lifetime's bitterness,

your fingers whispered
over my chest, moths skimming
a screen of skin

that let them taste
the light they craved
but wouldn't let them in.

The Eraser

has been busy again. This time
it's the sill, window
and horizon. My beads

are still there, holes cradled
in semi-precious skins,
but where's the cord

to string them? Table's
gone. The beads tremble. Nothing
holds them there. I see

the eraser now. It's working
on the air. Bold but somehow
childish strokes

erasing what we breathe.

The Pile of Bricks

Reminds you of your marriage.
      The rough rectangular burnt-clay tower
Stacked into a semblance

Of shelter
      Reminds you of the God,
Burnt and hardened,

Who reduced your marriage
      To a pile of bricks,
Of the concrete God

With holes in the middle
      You could stick your hand
Right through

If the holes in God,
      Like the holes in your marriage,
Weren't holes in you.

The Wind

Of worthlessness blows
The last three leaves
From the tree of the soul

Frozen like a woman
Holding a knife in a kitchen
Who doesn't run to see

If the screams she hears
Are the screams of her children
Because she doesn't remember

If she has children
To scream.

Winter Rain

December 23, 2007

No measuring what falls tonight.
Mercury rising,

The warmth of a lost season colliding
With the present tense of ice.

Rain climbs the concrete arteries of Manhattan,
Slicks the trenchcoats

Of sleepless mountains,
Licks the Connecticut

River's lips.
What will they cost,

These hours of rain?
Whose basement will flood,

Which hillsides vanish
Into warm blind sheets

Of pain? No rain like this
Has ever fallen.

If there is anything left between us,
This rain will wash it away.

The Leopard

for Yael

You are reporting on the leopard. You are only seven
And you already know the leopard
Comes in greys

As well as yellows. Tosses kills
Over branches. The leopard's children
Tumble in the shadow of a rock.

Gazelle bolt in the distance. Reporting on the leopard
Turns life and death
Into declarative sentences.

The gazelle ignores the leopard
Until the leopard snaps its neck.
In your kitchen love and hate

Shadow each other
The way you are shadowed
By the birthday that tiptoes closer.

You are only seven and you already know
You are the prey
Of the love you cannot escape. Love

Flings its kill over branches
In the jungle that is your kitchen.
You are only seven and you already know

Its spots will make love hard to see
Until it snaps your neck.

Loving Him

The lost father smiles down
From the snapshot summer
Where his children can always find him,

A past they try to see as a future
In which he has shed
The terrible skin

No one who loved him
Can bear to call his, least of all his children
Whose universe hangs

On the nail of the man
Dissolving before their eyes
Into a woman

Calling their names
In a voice they could only stand
When they didn't realize

It was speaking to them
As though in the loss
Of the man they loved

Love were traveling toward them.

Happily Ever After

For Yael—after we saw "Enchanted"

1

What is the objective now you ask.
You won't tell me what the objective is.

You insist I guess.
You don't get it do you you ask.

I don't. Happiness? *No.*
Love? *No.*

Whatever I imagine
You want is wrong.

You don't get it you say.
There is no objective.

2

The objective
Is to become real.

Wrong. In this film, reality is exile
Imposed by an evil queen

From a world in which animals
Come when you sing. You tumble

Down a well, climb
Through a manhole

Into a world whose moral
Is No Happy Endings.

A world where there are no mothers. Vermin
Come when you sing.

3

You lean closer.
The darkness flickers, the prince

Makes an ass of himself,
Curtains become a dress,

The world of Happily Ever After
Unhappily learns to navigate

The capital of despair.
The popcorn bag is empty.

It tastes weird you say.
You eat another kiss.

Maybe you've had enough I say.
No you answer,

Swallowing six.
The almost princess has chosen to bite

The poisoned apple
That will make her love

Forget it ever existed.
She's laid out on the couch.

You say
Look how pale she is.

Of course I whisper.
She's almost dead.

Fortunately, in this world
Almost dead

Turns out to be the perfect posture
For receiving true love's kiss.

4

The princess awakens, memory intact,
And grabs a sword

To battle the dragon
That pretended to be her mother.

You are smiling now. Your mouth
Stretches wide

In the silvery light. The princess climbs
Story after story.

She needs to stab something
And is ready to kill

Without a moment's hesitation
Whatever stands in the way

Of happily ever after.

Spring

Once you have no home,
It's as if you never had one. Trees

Dangle dense green flags,
Patriotic displays

Of loyalty to the life
They root in. Home is nothing

But the years inside them,
Dark rings marking

Growth that was overtaken.

Letter

Life begins to speak to you again
like an unanswered letter
carried for years in your bag

beneath lipsticks and tickets
and the refrigerator magnet
shaped like a house

that's all of home you have. It isn't easy
to listen. Life claims
you've been unfaithful, though you swear

you don't remember the vow
life thinks you've broken.
Perhaps life has mistaken you for someone else,

someone who is
what you once were,
half-asleep, content

with a closetful
of miseries and happiness
that almost seem to fit.

Return Flight

July 6, 2008

You descend toward your life
It's summer there
The mud has dried in the driveway

The leaves are weeks thicker
So many boys and girls
Have fumbled toward each other

On so many overgrown paths
You thought you were living
At the bottom of a mountain

But now you see you are falling
Like the moon
Reflected in well water

Life is growing
Larger or is it closer
You can't see anything

But the half-circle of light
You thought had been swallowed
By the circle of night

Mizmor L'Todah (Psalm of Thanks)

I'm grateful for the squirrel
Crouched between leaves
That cling, in autumn, to green. Grateful
For the death that lights the future
Like a sun I cannot see.

I'm grateful for the creepers
The squirrel wades, hip-deep. Grateful
For the scarlet waters
Of leaves that have ceased to feed.
I'm grateful for the rocks

Vanished glaciers fractured. For the nut
That swells the squirrel's cheeks.
I'm grateful for the sun
That shines in other people.
For the psalm that swells in me.

The Game

for Gabriel, May 19, 2007

When you reach the final stair
The orb will be there.
The witch can't stop you, the octopus woman

Shakes eight impotent legs
As you fly past. Even the tree
Of life is shaken. Stars of power

Shiver in its branches
Waiting for you to reach them.
Nothing can stop you now,

Can keep you from flying
Into the future
Where the man you will become

Is reaching back
To touch the boy who flew
So far so fast. You arrive before

The future realizes
You are already there,
Shining faintly, like the stars

Tangled in your hair.

II.

Democracy is Burning

This sequence of poems is composed entirely of words drawn from articles published in *The New York Times* on the morning of September 11, 2001, and words found in chapters 9 and 11 of the Biblical book of Leviticus—chapters that delineate Bronze Age laws of purity and sacrifice. Each poem combines words drawn from two *Times* articles with words drawn from a passage found in either chapter 9 or chapter 11 of Leviticus. Thus, each poem fuses language that reflects the secular pre-9/11 attack world with language that represents a fundamentalist world in which God is served through blood, burning and sacrifice.

These poems draw on the following *New York Times* articles:

"Plotting an Aerial Attack on Marauding Fire Ants"
"4 are Charged in Beating at Youth Center"
"France's Shock Novelist Strikes Again"
"Old-Fashioned Poetry but a Wild Life"
"Celebrity Watching Vs. Films at Toronto Festival,"
"Candidate Expands the Assault on Spending Limits"
"Cheek to Muzzle, Hand to Paw at Doggie Disco"
"Arsenic Standard for Water is Too Lax, Study Concludes"
"Advertising"
"Vital Signs"
"Life and Death Stakes in the Numbers Game"
"4 are Charged in Beating at Youth Center"

Prologue: An Aerial Attack with a Religious Center

Winged nightmares flew in to slaughter.
This is the thing
God commanded them to do.

The slaughter was a gradual process. Blood poured
On the heart of the Heartland
As the nightmares flew

Toward the center
They had slaughtered, the thing, the God,
Burning on the altar. Even the nightmares

Must have suffered.
No one really knows. The nightmares
Couldn't be reached for comment, but struck

By the density of burning flesh, a student
Dipped his finger in the blood
And began mapping the invasion backward,

From the East Coast to Florida
To the innards of the Heartland
Blinded by smoke and fire. God appears

To converse in nightmares, flying backward
Between horns of slaughter,
Dipping His finger in the blood

Pouring over the foundations
Of the Heartland. The sons responsible
For protecting the center

Draw near the altar. Slaughter
May be the answer. No one
Knows. The Heartland

Cannot be reached for comment
And there is no listing for the fats,
Or the kidneys, or the diaphragms, or the livers,

Or the God
Going up in smoke on the altar.

1. Consuming Encounter

In the consuming encounter
Between our religion and theirs,
Between the religions that kill,

Shivering with monotheistic enthusiasm,
And the religions that shiver
Among the ironies of capitalism,

God is a gradual process
No one really knows, overshadowed
Or condemned to disappear,

Consumed by the fire
In which religions mutate
Into processes of terror, are dipped

In fundamentalist blood, go up in smoke
On the altar
As God burns across the earth,

A mortal animal shiver,
Consuming religions, ours and theirs,
With living outrage and pleasure.

2. Mouth-to-Mouth Resuscitation

Throngs began to gather
Near the epicenter,
Painstakingly reconstructing

Sidewalks and corridors
As if they wished the dead
To come alive again.

Stop the film, someone shouted,
But the film continued to play
Among the burning people.

The lights were turned up. Stop the future,
Someone said,
But the future continued to play,

Touching the sleeves
Of the sidewalk crowd, performing
Mouth-to-mouth resuscitation

On the God failing
At the epicenter. The future
Seemed curiously old-fashioned.

Maybe it was. The lights were turned up,
But death continued
To finger the crowd

Pouring like blood across the sidewalks
Toward the packed
Pathography of the future.

Come alive again, someone shouted,
Performing
Mouth-to-mouth rescuscitation

On the old-fashioned epicenter,
God,
Burning around his neck.

3. Democracy is Burning

Slaying and sacrificing
Who they were—who we were—
To what they stand for, the opponents of the future

Burn as a form
Of political expression.
The message of democracy

Seems as healthy, if not healthier,
Burning upon the altar.
In Denver, in Albuquerque, in Boston, in Vermont, sidewalks thick

With people in long-sleeved shirts
Burn for the democracy
Burning on the altar. To the opponents of the future,

Democracy is a city
That can be burned.
Democracy *is* a city. Crowded sidewalks,

Democracy's altars, fill with voters
Burning to sacrifice
Who they are

On the altar
Of what they stand for.

4. An Election

Is a touching dance. The leaders
Carry the carcasses
Cheek to cheek, their slow, reverent movements

Guiding the cameras in.
Whoever competes, whoever touches,
Whoever votes, whoever judges,

Dances. The Devil
Locks eyes with voters
In Los Angeles, in New York, in Boston,

And jumps on democracy's back. He likes
Democracy acting happy,
Clearly intimidated yet dancing

Among bones and carcasses. Democracy,
For all its carcasses and devils,
Is the greatest advance in human relations,

A stunning approximation of a moon,
A roar, a leap, an animal singing
About freedom of expression

On a retractable leash.

5. Evidence

Somebody—her face is wrapped in black—
Muses about the fire from God
Chaining the most explosive people

To the most explosive events. Government officials
Circle the altar
Of disaster, consumed

By cameras zooming in
On burning shoulders and breasts.
We fall on our faces

Before the evidence. God just stands there,
An altar of regret,
A justifying fire,

Part of the act.

6. Love

If we were smart, we would get back
To the peaceful almost-quiet
Of general reminiscence,

The intimate music
That romanticizes the burning
Without touching it, presenting the disaster

As a sensitive, personal,
Even moving situation
While closing the door

On the emotion branded
Like a lover's name
In our flesh. Love

Brings the burning close,
Touching the blood
To our fingers, hiding the blood

In our flesh. In stores, in art, in the fragrance
Of weddings and chocolate, love sounds
The joy we can almost touch, the peace

We can almost imagine,
Narrowing our choices,
Boxing us in, chaining

Our most intimate experiences
To public disaster. Dangerous, bloody,
The waters of love

Pour through the caul
Of political decisions
Targeted to protect

Our sensitive population
From the wave of blood
Outside the country, from the countries burning

To make us safe.

7. Vital Signs

They feel hot, the seas and the rivers.
Hot to the touch.
The fins and scales of abomination

Turn like a blind man's head
As you walk by. You don't aim
To eat of their flesh

But your inner body
Feels the carcasses
As you make your way

Through the obstacle course
Of multiple explanations.
That, they say, is to be expected.

You feel hot, hot to the touch,
But your body doesn't drop
Onto the scales

Of abomination. Explanation
Keeps you stable, balancing
The peaceful, intimate effects

Of closed eyes, chocolate, love at first sight,
All the things you do to feel,
Against the carcasses

That move in the waters
Of explanation.
Walking, dancing, hot to the touch, turning

Like a blind man's head
From the rivers
Of flesh,

You make your way
Through the sea of feeling
Feeling its way

Through your carcass.

8. Death

These days, it's all about death.
One or two deaths, reported deaths, levels of death, death
Chewing the cud of death. Death

Explains, death tests
The nebulous line
Between failure of heart

And failure of nerve
And failure to touch
The heart and nerve

Of death. Death
Is an intravenous experiment
That brings the nerves back

To the congestive heart
Of death. Death
Mimics our vital signs, continuously increasing

The spiritual pressure
Of the history
Of death. Death

Is lucky. In a field
In which there is little room
For error, death can afford to take chances

On psychological, spiritual, historical explanations
For our failure to lament
The higher-than-expected,

Winged and flying,
Congestive, retrospective
Industry of death.

Epilogue: The Heart of the Heartland

Death O Lord
Has become your altar,
Your religious center. The children we risk,

The children we offer,
Reflect the tremendous spiritual pressure
Created on the field of slaughter

To sit all night
In the blood pouring out
At the bottom of our hearts

To atone for burning
The children of blood who slay
And the children, our children,

Who slay them. O Lord,
Sit with us all night
In the congestion of our hearts,

In the blood and manure,
Burnt meat and burning oil
Of the peace we cannot reach. The heart

Of the Heartland
Is burning. Atone
For us, O Lord, and we

Will atone for you.

III.

Survival Guide

Today's Forecast:

Intermittent life
Followed by death. Tomorrow,
Patches of death

With a chance of desperation
Around midnight. Some accumulation
Is predicted.

Daylilies

For Nancy Mayer

Their orange lips droop
Like lips after love.
Their sexual parts are damp

Though no one
Has touched them.
Swallows of rain

Pool in the shadows
Of their stamens.
They cannot love

But their mouths are always open,
Rain-swallows linger
Among shadowy stamens

Vulgar and beautiful
As the sexual parts of horses,
Orange lips slicked

As the heart is slicked
By the rage
At the heart of compassion.

On the Train to Exeter

The advertising men behind me
worry how to explain
what it is they do. We need rain
at Wimbledon, one says. Uneasy laughter

from the other two. The college boy
across the aisle
lays his fashionably hollow cheek
on his girlfriend's ample lap.

The man beside me's
nodded off again. The ad men
search for verbs. It's the idea
we're selling, one of them insists,

his voice young, eager, worried
the others know he knows
he's diminished himself
to fit in with them, given up

on something he could have been,
something hidden
in the sheep-nibbled hills,
rickety bridges, trickles of water,

horizon as comfortable
as a broken-in shoe. Cows doze
in the tea-time sun, dreaming,
as he and I dream,

of the verbs asleep inside them.

Passing the Belgian Ambassador's Residence in Jerusalem

You walk slowly through the world
That slowly walks through you.

It isn't as peaceful as it sounds.
The wars you carry

Into the heart of the world
The world carries

On in yours. The whispering rivers
Of your blood

Are whispered
By the rivers of blood

Spilling over the world
That spills its sunlight into your mouth

Like the golden pulp
Of a golden fruit, licking

The lips you lick, dying to taste
One golden drop

Of the golden fountain
Of the world you walk.

Natural Disasters

Last night, tens
of thousands were buried alive
while I slept

well for the first time since—
well, since before that cyclone
sank a chunk of Burma. Bodies floating

like grains of rice. Not that I lost
sleep over that. This is where my candor
wins your respect—

the mention, in passing, stoicism underlining
emotion left unsaid,
of nightmares and nightsweats,

the loss of this and that,
my father's recent death. Recent?
Well, it was before the earthquakes

in the Phillipines, the Indonesian floods, the tsunami that swallowed
the Solomons. Somewhere among the natural disasters,
my father's equally natural death

became the worst thing that had happened to me
since his refusal
to acknowledge my existence

sank the shores of love
in what are still known, in these days
of near-apocalypse,

as emotional depths.

The Body of Life

Turns inside out. Internal organs
Hang like clouds.

Snap out of it. Life
Is not a body. Bodies

Are life. The young with blood
In their smiles, the old wrinkling

On the vines that root them
In the century gone by,

Your face magnified
In the train-window twilight,

Nose and pores, ridges above eyes,
A life, your life,

Speeding toward the only form
In which it can survive.

Now and Then

your old face reappears
fringed
with the close-cropped hair

she loved to run her fingers through
when the cut was fresh.
Scalp tingled where she touched.

Your old face flushed
beneath the fingers
running now

through another head. Your new face
squints into summer sun.
Beads with tears of sweat.

Door

The door to your room is open
But the door to you is closed.

I can't see what slammed you shut
But something of me is caught

In something of you
That keeps on slamming. Even you

Don't know why you're hiding
Behind the door

You can't stop closing
Or begging me

To open.

Dozing to Waterfall

Tears and muddy
White-brown tresses

Plunge over the bone ledge
Where skull becomes sleep

Whispering to herself
Like a girl

Hiding behind her hair,
Hoping no one is there

To notice the tears
Behind the bangs

Love parts slowly,
Inviting her to dance.

Seed

You plant a seed and all that grows
is another seed
you put in your pocket

You eat dinner get divorced
watch snow fall
on the life that's melted

into someone else's
The snow is gone
The seed is too

but when the lawn
breaks out in flowers
one of them is yours

Survival Guide

1. There

It's time to celebrate
The anatomy of There,
The difference, the exile

That's inside you,
More reliable than the life
You wish you hadn't made. There

Is there, between your emotions
And your fingertips,
Diverting your eyes

From the familiar, scary
Miracle of life
Kissing your hair, laughing

At your exile, touching you
There.

2. Being

You flirt with being
The you that survives
In the drizzling village of the self

You cheated of color and size,
The face alive
Beneath the ice

Of time, a not-so-obvious sign
That there still is a future
That still has the power

To whisper your name. Admit it:
You have a hard time
Being. You thought you didn't have

To be. You thought you could pretend to be
A few hours a day, could juggle pieces
Of the you

You weren't, the future
No one would ever meet. But being
Keeps calling

Out of sunlight and water, composing the you
You meant never to be
From parts of you the you you are

Signed away. You
Are made by being
Unmade. It's a natural process.

Don't be afraid.

3. Love Hangs

In the water
Like a tampon string.
As if that weren't embarrassing enough,

Love is in the room, watching you pull away
From the family
You think you've lost

In the water you just had to spill
To hydrate the future. But nothing
Gets lost in the water.

Even as you pull away, you are still responsible
For the love that spilled
Each version of you

Into the family whose love
Seemed to cancel your world,
And for the losses, theirs and yours,

Shining ethereally
In the heart of the water
Washing them back to you.

4. Survival Guide

No matter how old you are,
It helps to be young
When you're coming to life,

To be unfinished, a mysterious statement,
A journey from star to star,
So break out a box of Crayolas

And draw your family
Looking uncomfortably away
From the you you've exchanged

For the mannequin
They named. You *should*
Help clean up, but you're so busy being afraid

To love or not
You miss how fun it is to clothe yourself
In the embarrassment of life.

Frost your lids with midnight;
Lid your heart with frost;
Rub them all over, the hormones that regulate

The production of love
From karmic garbage dumps,
Turn yourself into

The real you
You can only discover
By being other.

Voila! You're free.
Learn to love the awkward silence
You are going to be.

IV.

Answer

Crèche

God,
Struggling to be born.

We'll have to cut
A midwife would murmur

But no one assists this birth,
There is no womb, no egg, no sperm,

No one who can conceive
The God the swollen universe

Is screaming to release.

The Grave of Craving

God named the place "The Graves of Craving"…
(Numbers 11:34)

The soul rises
From the grave of craving
Rose and is rising

Green shoots rise from the grave of craving
Yellow shoots thin white tendrils
Like the hair of the dead

Rose and are rising
Rising from the grave of craving
Toward a sun that sinks

Toward an Earth that rises
From craving unto craving
The heavens are sealed like a seed

The sun like a seed is smothered
But Earth Earth is rising
Rising from the grave of craving

Through living and dying
Toward an Earth and a heaven
Smothered and shining

Medallion Inscribed with the Hebrew Alphabet in the Shape of a Flame

Where unmarked, you mirror,
gilding as you reflect
the hollows beneath my eyes

as though you want me to prize
the glittering
flesh of time.

But of course, you couldn't care less
about surfaces, yours or mine. Your heart
is in the frozen blaze

of letters stamped
so deeply into your substance
my fingernail is arrested

at every border
between what means
and what reflects.

Your letters are what stops me;
your letters are what burns
and burnishes the void

on which God engraves the world.

God is Beating

Wings in August leaves.
The leaves are dusty; the wings are black;
Their beating a heart, terrified
Then free.

Touching the Tree of Life

There are holes in the leaves,
Parts of world and self

You've tried to escape,
Wounds that keep telling you

To get sick and die
Because you love too much.

You are a survivor of the worst
You can do, a myopic mirror,

A brokenhearted refrigerator,
A shrinking layer of ice

Between the losses calling you
To kill yourself

And the clairvoyant dreams of communion
In which you touch and are touched

By parents, siblings, generations
Who tried, like you, to escape

The erotic ecology of pain.
When you turn around, no one is there

But the holes in the leaves
You find yourself touching

In the tree of lives
You live.

Answer

Where the waters of death empty
Into the waters of life

The grass grows higher than your head.
The soil between your toes is damp.

You lost your shoes some ways back.
This is holy ground, the waters said

Or a voice you took
For the voice of the waters

Pulling you under
Time and again. You were trying

To learn to walk
When you needed to learn to swim. You part

The grass that whispers
Through the waters that sing in your ears.

You can't make out the question
So you answer Yes.

Va-yera

"And God appeared"—*the opening words of the weekly por-
tion of* Genesis *in which the aged Sarah gives birth to Isaac
and banishes Hagar and Ishmael to the wilderness*

I wake up loved. Nightmares again,
empty beds, fingers of darkness
fingering my skin. I wake up

soaking wet, pregnant with impossibility, ninety
years old and growing younger, more tender,
a lover's voice

lingering in my ear, bra dangling
over the back of a chair, empty cups
cupping emptiness. Sarah

suckling a son named Laughter
at her superannuated breast. Everyone
will laugh at me, she laughs.

The angel appears,
or was it always there?
I wake up loved. Here.

V.

Coming to Life

All words taken from *Cosmo Girl* Dec 2007 /Jan 2008

Coming to Life

It makes you desperate, turning
From a cartoon
Into a real–life girl

With animated locks
And a gigantic puffy heart. Life
Is your most elaborate costume yet,

A fairytale
You try to layer on
Without injuring yourself.

Happy or not, you are filling in.
The heart that tried
To keep you warm

Made you look old, rigid,
A powdery copy
Of a knowing smirk. Now you can almost taste

The dragonfly
Beauty of the world:
The budding face

Of something other, the music
Of worlds coming together, the pearl
Of perfectly created spirit

In mountains, olives, the strange
Angelic rain
Of ever after. Welcome

To the neverending luxury
Of being, of being
Nothing, of being endlessly

Ready to be. Don't be afraid
Of being nothing. You are
Nothing. Nothing

Is what it takes to be.

Hurting

You're hurting yourself again, wasting time
Remembering
How much of you has melted,

How many spoonfuls
Of body and soul
Have been beaten together

To serve the you
You shadow, the beautiful life
You're hurting.

You find yourself funnier
When you're hurting,
Darker, riper,

More interesting
Than the hurricane of beauty
That insists on making

Everything smell wonderful,
Tickling you from heels to shoulders,
Covering the kiss of pain. Pain

Is healthier for you than chocolate,
Sweeter than love,
The best of the emotions

Kicking serious booty
In your dreams. Pain
Likes you. You sit next to her

Whenever you can. Hurting
Is something the two of you
Have in common, an inside joke

That keeps you laughing together.
You fidget, flirting
With saying goodbye. Pain

Wants to show you something. Insists
You pay close attention
To her eyes. No matter how much

Or little you love,
According to pain,
You should be satisfied.

Mind

The mind keeps you warm
By punishing you into loving
Or leaving life.

How green you are.
You are the mind's
Perfect victim,

A narrow, impersonating hive
Unwinding along
The winding line

Between matter and mind. Pay close attention
To the mind.
It loves you, it loves you not.

How can you know?
How can you know
How far you've come,

How much you've burned away
Of the world you've made
Of the mind's emissions? Irresistible songs

Carpet with honey
The bedroom the mind
Chokes with glades

Of unsmelled roses
To keep you happy
As you are eliminated.

Half your mind is growing,
Half is smeared
Across the lips of the Earth

You haven't learned
To find. You take small steps
Through the smoke of the mind,

Following the anxious,
Sparkling smell
That is the fragrance

Of life.

The Slopes of Becoming

Just use powder.
Just use dust. Cover
Your extra-large pout

With charity, art, lust,
The scent of satin,
The crocodile shimmer of love.

Keep your back straight
As though you were rowing a boat
Toward the best of you

Across the icy slopes
Of becoming.
You don't have to be twenty-one

To be happy. You have eyes, princess,
Butter and velvet, virgin skin,
A village of softly vibrating wishes,

A choice
To narrow yourself
To a similarity, an ambience, a pair of panty hose,

Or to shuffle toward self-creation,
Carrying everywhere
The twitchy, panic-prone perspective

You fear is about to explode.
You return slowly, princess,
You slowly returns, praying silently

That you can pull
Your life from the ice
Of shouldn't that and shouldn't this

Into your breathing,
Into your fingertips.

Girl in a Bottle

You may have lost hope
But you are definitely a girl
Hope hasn't lost. The almond, orphaned scent

Of adolescence braids
Your life with unwanted features,
Shaving your head,

Raising the shades
That kept you nice and protected,
Celebrating

Your year of being nude, a crystal skull
Extended to full-size
For everyone to see.

The restless young light
That is always on
Pearls the little secrets

Of your body, misting the habits
That strand you
In the mirror. Reality

Lines up to smooch,
Bites your fingernails,
Whispers the secret signs

That can get you into the best parties—
Or are they anxieties
That only look like parties?—

Bullying, taking full advantage
Of your metamorphosis
Into a girl you don't even know. It's time

To fill in the blanks.
Which makeup will you choose?
Which conscience? Which version of family

Will take your breath away?
Your arms, your legs,
Whisper the world you always wanted,

Fashioning conscience
From your body's vulnerability.
You vowed to conceal

The hope whose strands
Made you real,
But you have been born

Into the streaming light of history,
A shyly confessional bliss,
Because you didn't have to live,

Girl in a bottle,
And did.

Coming True

You're not in any hurry
To come true. That's fine,
But time-consuming.

You've already got
A beautiful spiritual structure
You've never completed,

And a mind that's overflowing
With love-sick whispers.
Your mystical side

Is getting bored. Perfection
May be unreachable,
But finding the focus necessary

To enter the stranded
Blessing of the body
Is still your responsibility.

Even when change gets tough,
The future is running toward you,
A golden shadow, a sibling, a long-lost crush.

You've both matured, so you can be sure
Things will be different now. Now that you want
To stick around, you can't avoid the truth:

It's time, past time,
To take life into your own hands
As life has taken you.

Kiss Everything

You only have 24 hours
To kiss everything, princess. The rabidly
Gorgeous locks

Of the knowledge
That you will die
Pulse in you,

Infesting your cheeks with midnight,
Awakening you to the sound
Of your body's downward history.

One girl will die, princess.
One girl will silver in the rain.
One girl—will it be you?—

Will get to be you
In real life, venturing
Into the eerie spirals

Of love-smitten smoke
Dancing calmly amidst the chaos
That makes you want to die.

You have a good foundation, princess,
Full of melodies, ukeleles, trombones, folk-dancing choirs,
Outrageous mists and mountains

Spinning fabulously out of control.
The inconsolable wilderness
In which you are suspended

Is probation, not a life sentence. The freedom
That seems to exterminate everything—
That's your galaxy.

Even If You Want

Even if you want
Absolutely nothing, you have to admit
You're adorably put together.

What were the odds of being
This triangle of expectations, doubts and love?
Others feel the same,

Too fraudulent, too fat, too addicted
To tortured relationships
With existence. Even if you want

Absolutely nothing—
But you can't want nothing. Existence
Might be fun, you think,

Goofy yet smart, calling you mom
When it's sure it's ruined,
Calling you lover

When you laugh at it for being
Its own harshest critic.
It's nice to exist, to laugh,

To be written off
And survive, born and reborn, to dream
You've made something

Of your imperfections,
To realize you don't have to be good
To make the world a place inside you

As you make a place
In the world. It's nice to fail your family
And it's nice to save them

By refusing to give up
The difference that made you
Fail. It's nice to want absolutely nothing,

And it's nice to be wanted,
To find yourself at home,
A visionary design

For some trivial object
That helps the world
To bloom.

Fairy Tale Ending

Now that you've graduated
From being abducted
For decades, you realize there are people

Exactly like you
Except that they happened to be born,
People who lead

And follow you
Toward something more human
Than self or personality.

You aren't just making
A self. Your self is a reflection
With oversized, glossy eyes

Of the face
Of a crisis, a civil war
Which is the only kind of love story

People who are displaced
Can manage. At times
You are scared for your life,

That it will be forced to serve
Children you can't expect
To know or care about you,

Children you have, children you were,
Children who need you
To feel real enough

To live. That's what you signed up for,
But they – the displacement
You put a face on

Is worse than they can imagine,
An existential seizure
That went on for decades.

You died, princess, and you live—
That's your fairy-tale ending.
You chained yourself to life

When you couldn't escape, when it felt
Like unbelievable cruelty
To accept that death

Was a journey you couldn't take
Without drilling
Through the people around you.

You are alive
Because you want
To be. That's all they know,

And all they need to know,
The children you had
And the child you were,

To live happily
Ever after.

Thickening

How dramatic you look
In the rich purple shadow
Of your life. You've never been

So happy
To be orphaned, blown away
In a storm of rapture

That seems to express
Who you are. Suddenly,
You exist for a purpose.

Your unbelievable confidence
That you can escape the skin
That felt so ugly

And still become yourself
Changes the people around you.
Hazy chains

Of flush and decay
Brush the apples
Of your cheeks,

A coy, metallic summer pigment
Shines through the creases
Of your wintry skin. You wish

You could glow like this forever,
Ringing in the darkness
Like a candle

From a better world, a cool sanctuary
From the pain
That blazes so fiercely right now,

Lighting up the morning
You've borrowed from the night.
Pewter, coral, champagne,

Abandoned before breakfast
Or blushing with life,
You are the woman you've shadowed,

The home you thought you'd lost,
The cartoon princess who remembers
Thickening into truth, and soon will remember

Being created anew.

Joy Ladin's previous books include *Alternatives to History*, *The Book of Anna, Transmigration* (a finalist for a 2009 Lambda Literary Award) and *Psalms*. She has been the recipient of a Fulbright Scholarship, an American Council of Learned Societies Fellowship, and a nomination for Pushcart Prize in Poetry. Ladin is currently working on a study of American modernist poetics while writing a memoir called *Inside Out: Confessions of a Woman Caught in the Act of Becoming*. She is David and Ruth Gottesman Professor of English at Stern College of Yeshiva University.